First Steps out

Why this book?

Have you ever w............ oved one, might have a drinking problem?

Do you ever find yourself…

- forgetting how many you've had?

- "just finishing off the bottle"?

If so, this book will help you understand:

- when drinking becomes a problem;

- how many people it affects, and in what way;

- what to do if you want to change – whether for the first time, or the fifth;

- how to set realistic goals and achieve them;

- how to avoid relapse;

- how to provide support to a problem drinker.

Full of tried-and-tested advice, it will enable you to take the first steps on the journey out of problem drinking – to a healthier, happier you.

*This book is dedicated
to my parents John and Cissie*

First Steps out of Problem Drinking

John McMahon

LION

Copyright © 2010 John McMahon
This edition copyright © 2010 Lion Hudson
The author asserts the moral right
to be identified as the author of this work

A Lion Book
an imprint of
Lion Hudson plc
Wilkinson House, Jordan Hill Road,
Oxford OX2 8DR, England
www.lionhudson.com
ISBN 978 0 7459 5397 7

Distributed by:
UK: Marston Book Services, PO Box 269,
Abingdon, Oxon, OX14 4YN
USA: Trafalgar Square Publishing, 814
N. Franklin Street, Chicago, IL 60610
USA Christian Market: Kregel Publications,
PO Box 2607, Grand Rapids, MI 49501
First edition 2010
10 9 8 7 6 5 4 3 2 1 0
All rights reserved

A catalogue record for this book is available
from the British Library
Typeset in 10.5/14 ITC Stone Serif
Printed and bound in Malta

Contents

Introduction

For decades it was believed that the only way out of addictive behaviours was to get treatment or attend Alcoholics Anonymous (AA). This view is now changing; in recent years it has been increasingly recognized that people with addiction problems can and do recover without the aid of treatment (including AA). At first it was thought that these people were the exception, that this so-called "natural recovery" was a rare phenomenon. However, research has found that rather than being rare, natural recovery is by far the most common route out of all kinds of addiction – smoking, drugs (including heroin), and alcohol.

Research on natural recovery has found that if people want to change their addictive behaviour for the better, then there are some basic steps that need to be carried out. This approach suggests that recovery from addiction is simple, but that should not be confused with "easy". There is no doubt that recovery is difficult and requires a lot of effort and persistence.

Don't be fooled by advertisements promising that

you can overcome your addiction in five minutes or by playing a CD while you are sleeping, or any other "get recovered quick" schemes. They may be tempting; in fact, they are *very* tempting – human nature is always looking for an easy way of doing things – but unfortunately they rarely, if ever, work.

However, if you follow the method laid out in this book, then there is a strong probability that you will be able to change your behaviour and lead a sober life.

Who is this book for?

This book is for anyone who knows, thinks, or even worries that they have a problem with alcohol. If you want to stop drinking, have a break from drinking, reduce drinking, or give your drinking a reality check, then this book can help you.

How many people are affected?

Approximately 8.2 million people in England alone – 26 per cent of adults (38 per cent of men, 16 per cent of women).
Approximately 1.1 million people in England are alcohol-dependent – 3.6 per cent of adults (6 per cent of men and 2 per cent of women).

Do you worry about your drinking? Do you sometimes, or even often, feel that you are drinking more than is good for you? Have others remarked about your drinking – your spouse, friends, boss? Do you regularly find yourself drinking more than you intended to, despite having promised yourself that it would not happen this time? Have you tried to cut down your drinking and failed? This book can help you.

It will provide you with a few simple tools that will allow you to assess whether or not you have a drinking problem and how that problem might be affecting your life. It will then show you how to use that assessment to build the motivation you need to change and maintain that change successfully. It will introduce you to simple strategies to avoid putting yourself at risk of relapsing, but if you do relapse, then this is also covered. Finally, it discusses issues that can arise when you change, and finishes with a chapter for your family or those who are supporting you.

How do I use this book?

Getting sober is no different from any other task. The preparation is the most important part. Take your time and do it properly and the rest of the work should go smoothly; do it in a rushed or shoddy fashion and you are likely to struggle.

When changing your behaviour, the more information you have about the behaviour, the easier it will be. At a basic level, you need to know what it is that you are changing and why.

In this book are the tools for a new life, but they will not change your life unless you put them to use. If you do use the tools wisely, your life will be so different,

and alcohol will no longer be a problem for you or your family.

Over to you!

Reading this book will no more get you sober than reading a fitness book will make you fit. It is what you do with the information that can change your future. You should use this book as a workbook and carry out the exercises and use the tools. You are the one who can get you sober – this book just shows you the way.

Why listen to me?

I come to this issue from many different perspectives. I have worked as a therapist in alcohol and drug treatment centres, where I have treated people and created new treatment programmes. For twenty years I was an academic researching how people change, and I have published widely and presented at conferences all over the world. During that time I helped to write and teach the biggest master's level course on addiction in the UK. More recently, I have designed and created successful self-help websites – one, which won an award, to help people with an alcohol problem, another for their families – and I was commissioned to build the alcohol website for a major health board.

But alongside these professional reasons there is a personal one. I've been there! I had a major problem with alcohol and drugs, which required me to be hospitalized at one stage. I have now been clean and sober for more than twenty-five years (since 1984). So if you put all that experience together, I just may have some insight into where you are coming from and where you are going.

Good reading and good luck.

John

1

Drinking problems – clinical perspectives

One evening I got a phone call. It came from a woman who was worried about her grown-up son. He was at her house after splitting from his wife and he had been drinking heavily for a few days. I said that I would call round the next morning and that she should try to prevent him from drinking any more that night. I called round the next day and was shown into his bedroom. He lay in bed, clearly in a poor state. He was shaking, sweating, and obviously withdrawing from alcohol. His first words to me were, "I'm not an alcoholic."

I had not mentioned the word "alcoholic", but nevertheless he had to make it clear to me that he was not one. To most people, including his mother, he clearly fitted the "alcoholic" label. But if he was going to accept help, then it had to be on the understanding that he was not an alcoholic.

People who may have an alcohol problem often say, "I'm not an alcoholic." This is not necessarily to excuse or minimize the severity of their problem, but rather to avoid the stigma and shame that appears to be attached to that label. Despite estimates that suggest that around 1 million people in the UK have a serious alcohol problem, the word "alcoholic" still has negative power. Having to admit to being an alcoholic is such a barrier to getting help that nowadays it is rarely a precondition of treatment.

Current thinking in medical and treatment circles also suggests the term "alcoholic" is too emotionally and value laden to be useful. For this reason it is no longer in common usage in medical circles. Instead, the terms that tend to be used today are "binge drinking", "alcohol abuse", and "alcohol dependence". These terms are defined below.

Mythbuster

You need to label yourself an "alcoholic" in order to recover.
No! It is, however, a requirement to recognize that alcohol is causing you a problem.

Categorizing alcohol problems

Binge drinking

Binge drinking was once a term applied to the behaviour of dependent drinkers who would drink steadily for days, or even weeks, at a time. This term is currently used for any drinking that is twice the recommended limits – two to three units per day for a female and three to four units per day for a male. In other words, daily consumption of more than six units for females and eight units for males would be considered to be binge drinking. You may think that this is not a great deal of alcohol and many would agree. However, if you are drinking this amount or more on a regular basis, then you are putting your health at risk.

Alcohol abuse

Alcohol abuse is a pattern of persistent heavy drinking that has regular negative consequences such as:

- failing to turn up at work, fulfil commitments, or keep appointments

- continually drinking in situations that could be dangerous – while in charge of a car or using machinery

- recurring legal problems – for example, arrest for disorderly conduct

 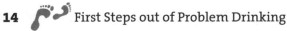

- serious and ongoing social problems - for example, marital difficulties.

Alcohol dependence

Alcohol dependence is also a pattern of heavy drinking, but someone is dependent if they meet three or more of the following seven criteria at any time over a year:

1. Increased tolerance – do you need more alcohol to get the same effect?

2. Withdrawal – do you shake, sweat, feel anxious, and use alcohol to relieve symptoms?

3. Impaired control – do you drink more alcohol and for longer than you intended?

4. Do you crave alcohol or have unsuccessful efforts to cut down or control alcohol use?

5. Do you spend a great deal of time trying to get alcohol, drinking, or having hangovers?

6. Have you given up social, occupational, or recreational activities to drink?

7. Have you continued to use alcohol despite having a persistent or recurrent physical or psychological problem that is likely to have been caused or exacerbated by the alcohol (for example, continued drinking even though you know that an ulcer was made worse by alcohol consumption)?

As you can see from the above definitions, the criterion for binge drinking is simply about exceeding the limits, whereas alcohol abuse is more about reckless use that disregards consequences. Dependence, however, is about the *need* to drink and the physiological and social changes that appear to be occurring. This term "dependence" tends to be used instead of "alcoholism".

Units of alcohol

Alcohol consumption is measured in units of alcohol because it is the quantity of alcohol consumed that is important, not the type of alcohol.

One unit =
half a pint of normal beer
a pub measure of spirits
one glass of table wine

So how do I know if I fit into a problem drinker category?

The first step in discovering if you are a problem drinker is to look at how much you drink – and to try to be as accurate as possible. Below you will find a seven-day drink diary to record your drinking for the previous week. This will give you a picture of your drinking pattern, frequency, and amount. However, if the previous week has not been typical – if you have consumed much more or much less than usual – then complete the diary for a recent more typical drinking week.

Start with today and work backwards. So write what you have had today and enter your drinking for the day in units, then do yesterday's, continuing until you have completed the drinking diary. Now it's time to assess your drinking pattern. Look at each day and see whether you consumed alcohol on that day or not.

- How many days did you drink? Are there any days you did not drink?

- Are there any days when you exceeded the recommended daily limits (three units for a female, four units for a male)? How many?

- Are there any days when you were bingeing (more than six units for a female or eight for a male)? How many?

Now add up the units for your week and put the total in the end column.

- Have you exceeded the recommended weekly limits (fourteen for female, twenty-one for male)? If you have exceeded the limits, then by how much? Is this your normal pattern of drinking?

Day	day	day	day	day	day	day	day	
Units								Total

From the information you have entered in this drink diary, you can easily tell whether or not you fit the category of binge drinking and the extent to which you are binge drinking. We shall now turn to an assessment that will enable you to decide whether you fit the category of alcohol abuse.

FAST

FAST is a questionnaire used to screen for alcohol abuse. It takes less than a minute to complete and is our next step on the way to recovery.

FAST Questionnaire

1. MEN: How often do you have **eight** or more drinks on one occasion?

   WOMEN: How often do you have **six** or more drinks on one occasion?

Never (0)	Less than monthly (1)	Monthly (2)	Weekly (3)	Daily or almost daily (4)

2. How often during the last year have you been unable to remember what happened the night before because you had been drinking?

Never (0)	Less than monthly (1)	Monthly (2)	Weekly (3)	Daily or almost daily (4)

3. How often during the last year have you failed to do what was normally expected of you because of drinking?

Never (0)	Less than monthly (1)	Monthly (2)	Weekly (3)	Daily or almost daily (4)

4. In the last year has a relative or friend, or a doctor or other health worker been concerned about your drinking or suggested you cut down?

No (0)	Yes, on one occasion (2)	Yes, on more than one occasion (4)

Score questions 1–3: 0, 1, 2, 3, 4.
Score question 4: 0, 2, 4.

Total score:_____

Scoring FAST

In question 1, if you answered "Never", then you are not misusing alcohol. If you answered "Weekly" or "Daily or almost daily", you are showing signs of bingeing, abuse, or dependency.

If the score for all four questions is less than three, then you may be bingeing occasionally but you are not abusing alcohol.

If the score for all four questions is more than three, then you are showing signs of alcohol abuse. The highest possible score for this questionnaire is sixteen. The closer your score is to sixteen, the more of a problem your drinking is and the more likely you are to be dependent on alcohol.

How did you score? Does this assessment suggest that you have a problem with your drinking? Does it increase your desire to change your drinking habits?

In the next chapter we will look at different methods of assessing your drinking – methods that are perhaps more fitting for a self-changer like you.

2

Self-assessment

In the previous chapter we looked at clinical methods of assessing your drinking. In this chapter we will take a more pragmatic and personal approach.

Most people don't need a medical diagnosis to tell them whether they have a drinking problem or not. Normally we know that ourselves – or our family, friends, or boss will tell us. The real acid test is the impact that drinking has on your life – all aspects of it. Later in this chapter we will consider how to assess the impact of alcohol, but first let's look at the symptoms of an alcohol problem.

Assessing your drinking

If you are engaging on a regular basis in at least three of the behaviours described below, you probably have an alcohol problem. Obviously, the more of these behaviours you indulge in and the more frequently you do so, the more likely you are to have a drinking problem.

- **Do you usually drink more than your friends?**

- **Do you hide how much you drink?** This can take many forms – sneaking extra drinks when you think no one is looking or carrying your own supply to top up your drink. You may hide alcohol in the house or put bottles in neighbours' bins to conceal how much you drink.

- **Do you regularly drink more than you intended?** Good intentions seem to be eroded and intended limits go by the wayside as you get drunk again.

- **Do you lie about how much you drink?**

- **Do you find it increasingly difficult to function without a drink?** Many people find socializing easier if they have a drink, but most can have a good time without alcohol. Can you?

- **Do you find it increasingly difficult to abstain from drinking? Do you find yourself drinking when you would not normally have had a drink previously?** Perhaps a shopping trip that would have included a coffee break might now have a wine break.

- **Are you experiencing more frequent and severe withdrawal symptoms?** These symptoms might include tremors (hands shaking) or sweating.

- **Are you experiencing anxiety and guilt feelings in the morning?** These feelings can exacerbate the shakes, and, conversely, anxiety can exacerbate the shakes and escalate to panic attacks.

- **Have you started having a morning drink?** A common way to try to alleviate such bad feelings is to take a little drink – hair of the dog that bit you.

How many of these behaviours do you identify in your drinking life? You may initially have the feeling of a behaviour (drinking) that is slipping out of control, just a little bit to begin with. Normally, a drinker feels that they could control their behaviour any time they wanted to, normally tomorrow rather than today. Sometimes they succeed. But often they don't and then drinking seems to take over and problems accelerate. If you feel that this is what is happening to you, then you probably have a problem.

Mythbuster

People who can hold their booze are to be admired.
No! This might indicate a developed tolerance and the onset of alcohol dependence.

Assessing the impact of drinking on your life

Another way to assess whether or not you have an alcohol problem is to examine the actual consequences of drinking. When people think about this, they tend to think of the health consequences. However, the effects of problem drinking are much broader than health alone and can affect all parts of your life, relationships, work, and leisure.

> **Alcohol affects all bodily functions, including:**
>
> - Brain – memory and understanding.
> - Heart – blood pressure and heart attacks.
> - Liver – cirrhosis.
> - Sexual – impotence.
> - Oesophagus and stomach – cancers.
> - Nerves – numbness.
>
> … and many more.

The consequences that you experience are often much more than merely the effects of alcohol. Indeed, many of the consequences are due to the behaviour that accompanies drinking. For example, if Tom spends every night in the pub, then he will have little time for his wife or family, and that could cause relationship problems through neglect. The amount of alcohol consumed is almost irrelevant; it is the fact that he is never home to build relationships or to help around the house that is the main issue.

Obviously, this problem is alcohol-related and it would be foolish to look at problems or issues in isolation. Nevertheless, that is what many alcohol assessments do: they focus only on the consumption and not on the accompanying behaviours. To get a clearer picture, this last assessment will introduce you to a more holistic approach. It considers the consequences of your personal drinking, and therefore the harm and the extent of the problem. This method is useful in later chapters because it gives you a tool to build your motivation to change, as well as an evaluation method of your recovery.

> **Mythbuster**

Alcohol gives you energy.
No! Alcohol is a depressant and actually makes you sleepy.

The four Wels

Since the effects of drinking can touch every part of a person's life, it can be difficult to make an accurate assessment of the level of the problem. Where do you start? What do you focus on? There is also the issue of individual attitudes and circumstances – what is a problem for one person might not be a problem for another.

To illustrate this point, let me tell you about a client I had many years ago. I was fairly new to alcohol counselling and worked in an alcohol unit in a large psychiatric hospital. Many of the clients there were at the severe end of the spectrum of alcohol problems. One day the police brought in a little old man for admission. He had thrown a brick through the window of a Marks & Spencer store in one of Glasgow's busiest streets and stolen two shirts.

I sat with the client and discussed his drinking, pointing out the problems that it had caused in his life. I explained at length that he would be going to prison again and suggested that this might be a very good reason to give up drinking. He just looked at me with a slightly patronizing stare and said, "Son, I'm homeless. I live on the streets and have done for years. Winter is coming and it gets too cold to be outdoors. If I go to prison, I get a bed in the warmth, three meals a day, and I see some old friends." Although, for me, going to prison would be a real deterrent to drinking, for him, prison was a good outcome. It actually helped him to survive the winter.

I learned a very valuable lesson that day: what motivates people is not the same in every case. Motivation is very individualized, which is why the following assessment is so useful. It uses your own assessment of what is happening in your life. It is not a tick list or a pre-prepared questionnaire. *You* create the list of issues and *you* decide on the extent of the problem each issue represents to you.

If you carry out a holistic assessment, then what is

required is a tool that is focused enough to guide you but flexible enough to be able to capture the issues of anyone. This is the four Wels, a simple but powerful tool to capture your issues. Each "Wel" represents an area of your life:

• **Well-being** – your health.

• **Wealth** – your finances and work-related issues.

• **Welcome** – your relationships.

• **Welfare** – other aspects of your life (for example, leisure or spirituality).

So how do you use this tool?

Over to you!
Using the four Wels

Before you start this exercise, gather together some A4 paper, a pen, and some highlighter pens – one green, one orange, and one red. Then find a quiet place where you will not be disturbed for an hour.

Take the paper and draw a cross on it to divide it into four equal segments. At the top of the upper left segment write "Well-being", in the upper right segment write "Wealth", in the bottom left write "Welcome", and in the bottom right segment write "Welfare". You are now ready to carry out your assessment.

Think about each area of your life and any concerns you have. If there are any concerns that spring immediately to mind, write them down as you think of them. You should also write down any concerns that others (for example, your spouse, boss, friends) have raised about your drinking. Do not try to censor or assess the impact of the issues at this stage. That comes later.

- **Well-being** – Consider your health and write down any health-related issues that you are concerned about, especially if they are, or you think they may be, alcohol-related. These might be gastric problems, psychological or mood problems, sexual problems.
- **Wealth** – Consider your finances and again write down anything that comes to mind. Common issues to think about are debt, cash flow, lost jobs.
- **Welcome** – Consider your relationships, family, and friends. Write down any alcohol-related issues you can think of.
- **Welfare** – Consider other spheres of your life such as how fulfilled you feel. Is your life what you hoped it would be? Does it have meaning? Do you have hobbies?

When you have finished filling in the page, it is time to make an assessment of each concern. Look at each concern that you have written down and decide if it is a small concern or no concern at all, a medium concern, or a major concern. With your highlighter pens mark each concern using a traffic light system: green for little or no concern, orange for a medium concern, and red for a major concern.

Reading the assessment

Now as you look at the paper it should be quite obvious
- whether there are major concerns in your life associated with drinking;
- how many major concerns there are;
- and in which areas of your life the majority of problems lie.

If you have not written any concerns in any of the areas of your life, or if any that you have written are highlighted green, then it would suggest that you feel that there is no problem with your drinking and that change is not required.

If the concerns are a mixture of orange and green, you may have some moderate concerns but still feel that little or no change is required.

If, however, there is even one concern highlighted in red on your page, then it is clear that you have at least one major issue that requires a change in drinking behaviour.

Hold on to this assessment, as you will use it again later.

3

Building motivation for change

Few of us wake up one morning and decide for no reason to change our lives, job, country, or drinking pattern. Humans are not built that way. Most of us like to have some permanence and routine. Imagine for a moment what the world would be like if there was no routine, no order, and no permanence. We would not be able to predict or anticipate anything. The sun might or might not come up in the morning; people would drive their cars on any side of the road they felt like; you might or might not have the job you had yesterday; the word "Hello" might be a challenge to fight today. You get the idea – chaos!

Motivation – positive and negative

As humans, we generally don't like change. We think that staying the same means things are OK; change means they're not. Well, this is not entirely true: sometimes change means "better". Advertisers play on this fact – "Buy this washing powder and your life will be transformed" or "Drink this coffee and it will feel like living in luxury". This is called "positive motivation", wanting to change to get something good. Although it doesn't always feel like it, most of us go to work because of positive motivation – money! The boss pays us money, so we turn up. If the boss stopped paying us money, how many of us would continue to turn up?

Another type of motivation is "negative motivation". This is when we change to avoid or stop something bad happening – for example, driving slowly past a speed camera, avoiding dangerous areas of the city at night, or not eating a food that we know will make us ill. Some psychologists argue that all behaviour, including change, can be explained by the motivations we have in our lives.

How is this relevant to changing your drinking behaviour? Well, current thinking in addiction suggests that motivation is at the heart of it. Simply put, people are motivated to drink because they want to get good things – feel good, confident, relaxed – and they are motivated to change to avoid the bad things – feeling bad, health problems, relationship problems.

I want to change because…
- *"I want to see my children grow up."*
- *"I don't want to lose my marriage."*
- *"I am worried about my health."*
- *"I am ashamed of the way I behave when drinking."*
- *"I feel that I am losing control of drinking."*

So, if you are going to be successful in changing your drinking behaviour, your motivation to change must be stronger than your motivation to drink. This includes not only initiating change but also maintaining it. Mark Twain is reputed to have said, "Quitting smoking is easy. I've done it hundreds of times." The point is that it may be easy to stop but it's not so easy to stay stopped.

Areas of concern revisited

The assessment from the last chapter can now be of enormous value to you. The problems you identified are the reasons why you want to change your drinking behaviour: to reduce or, preferably, eliminate these problems. For example, if you have been threatened with the sack from your job, then this is a clear incentive to change; and if your spouse has threatened to leave, again that's an incentive to change. So that assessment can be your biggest asset in changing.

Over to you!

Revisit the assessment and decide where the majority of the problems lie – well-being, wealth, welcome, or welfare. This shows you which area of your life is most affected or you are most concerned about. Remember that it is not just the number of problems that matters. There can be many small problems which, although undesirable, have little effect on behaviour. On the other hand, one major problem can provide an enormous boost in motivation to help you through the low times that can lead to relapse.

On your own assessment:

- Are there any particular concerns that stand out for you?
- Is there a concern that makes you say, "I do not want this to continue, I want to change"?
- Or is there a whole collection of concerns that makes your life difficult and makes you want to change?

Write these concerns down on a card, a piece of paper, your diary, the desktop of your computer, or all of these. Stick the paper on the fridge, above your workstation, or on your bedroom mirror; put it in your wallet. These concerns provide your motivation and you need to remind yourself on a regular basis of why you are changing.

There will be days when your mind whispers, "I'm not that bad… it's not that much of a problem… maybe it would be OK to drink again." This is something that we will discuss at more length in Chapter 8. Having a card or piece of paper that is always with you is a regular reminder and can help maintain your motivation. However, having that piece of paper with you will not help if you do not read it. Starting the day with a reminder will put you in the right frame of mind to have a successful day.

Pros and cons

Another useful exercise in building motivation is to look at the consequences, both good and bad, that come from changing or not changing your behaviour.

Over to you!

You need some A4 paper, a pen, and a quiet place where you will not be interrupted for half an hour. Start by drawing a cross on the paper to divide the paper into four equal segments. Across the top of the page, for the top two segments, write "Pros" and below the centre, for the bottom two segments, write "Cons". At the top of the paper on the left side write "No change", and on the right side write "Change". You are now ready to carry out the exercise.

In the top left segment list the pros of no change – all the good things about your current drinking habit, things that you like about drinking. You might list feelings, company, freedom – include anything good about your drinking.

In the segment below, list the cons of no change. These will include the things about your drinking that you do not enjoy. They may be some or all of the consequences that you listed in the areas of concern exercise.

Now look at the pros and cons of change in the other segments. In order to make this exercise meaningful, you need to approach it with a very definite idea of what your goal of change will be. For example, you might decide that you want to be abstinent or you might want to reduce your drinking. Obviously the pros and cons of these goals could be very different. You can use this technique to compare the pros and cons of the different goals.

Often, people who have been drinking heavily for many years find it difficult to think of anything for the pros of change. All they can think of is that the bad outcomes will be reduced or eradicated. However, there may be many things you could include in this segment. For example, is there a hobby, sport, or pastime that you have dreamed of doing but you have never had the time? If you saved the money you spent on alcohol, is there something special that you would like to buy for you, your spouse, or your children? Or perhaps you might want to study or learn a new skill?

What you include in this section will be very different if you view this as an opportunity rather than a loss. For many people who have changed their drinking habits, it has indeed been an opportunity to change their whole life and outlook, and many of them have gone on to have a better life than they ever thought possible.

Victim or victor?

Some victors I know

- A woman who has opened many businesses and is a millionaire.
- A man who says he is happier than ever and saw his grandson born.

How you approach change can be an important factor in whether or not you are successful. If, like many people, you approach it with the attitude that you are a victim and that alcohol is being taken away from you, you will find it very difficult to cope when your other defences are low and you are craving a drink.

Instead, you can approach this as an opportunity to do something different, to achieve something that you have dreamed about doing for years. This is a much more positive attitude and it may carry you through the hard times. In research, people who have recovered from addictions have described their struggle to change in a number of different "recovery stories". However, one thing is generally clear in all of them: they see themselves as the hero of the story, not the victim. One story is reminiscent of St George slaying the dragon; another is about an escape from slavery. The point is that the people involved see change and recovery as a very positive move, not a negative one. They are victors exercising a positive choice, not victims being denied their pleasure.

So try to be positive and see change as an opportunity, and the process will be much easier and more likely to be successful.

4

Setting your goal

In Chapters 1 and 2 you assessed the extent of your drinking problem, and in Chapter 3 you started to build motivation for change. In this chapter you will start your process of change by making a decision about your drinking goal.

Obviously, you need to decide on that goal. Should you aim for abstinence, controlled drinking, or reduced drinking? Most people, given the choice, will opt to aim for controlled drinking or reduced drinking. Abstinence is rarely the first goal of choice, unless you have tried in the past to control your drinking or the negatives of drinking have been very severe. However, putting aside your first choice or your history for the moment, let us look at some guidelines that may inform your choice of goal.

Goals

When making a decision about your drinking goal, you should take a close and honest look at the assessments you have carried out. If your assessments have any of the following characteristics, you should seriously consider at least a temporary period of abstinence:

- You scored six or more on the FAST questionnaire.

- Your "areas of concern" assessment had severe (red) problems in the "Well-being" category.

- Your "areas of concern" assessment had severe (red) problems in the "Welcome" category related to your family and/or partner.

- You are showing signs of dependency (for example, withdrawal).

A temporary period of abstinence can be a very useful strategy to begin the change process. Research has shown that those who successfully maintain abstinence for a short time are more successful in the long run for the following reasons:

- First, abstaining reduces tolerance, so alcohol has a greater effect at lower doses.

- Second, abstaining allows cognitive abilities dulled by alcohol to improve significantly.

- Third, abstaining allows you to begin to deal with temptations, craving, and social pressure to drink.

Normally, a period of temporary abstinence of between one and three months is recommended. I prefer three months. When people drink heavily, often there is a habitual aspect to the drinking. Habits take time to break and so does establishing new and healthier habits.

Up until a few years ago I was a smoker. I smoked in my car as I drove to work, and every morning as I passed a particular landmark I would light a cigarette. This landmark marked the final leg of my commute and this was my last cigarette before entering work. Long after I gave up smoking I still felt a strong urge to smoke when I passed this landmark. It took a long time for this association to go away.

It is the same with drinking. There are places, people, situations, and feelings that are associated with drinking. It takes time for these associations to weaken so that you can gain more control over alcohol.

A period of abstinence also gives you time to mull over your assessments, and perhaps to reduce some of the difficulties that may be happening at home, so that new relationships can be forged and old relationships can be repaired. Physically, it also gives your body time to repair and heal alcohol-related damage.

Some people who have completed a three-month temporary abstinence find that they are quite happy as non-drinkers and continue in an abstinent status. Others go back to drinking but on a reduced basis.

The temporary abstinence is not compulsory but it is strongly recommended.

So, now it is time to choose your goal:

- abstinence

- controlled drinking

- reduced drinking.

Abstinence

Although any goal must be the individual's choice, abstinence is sometimes strongly indicated by the assessment. For example, in cases where there is severe liver damage and further consumption of alcohol will only exacerbate the problem, stopping drinking is strongly recommended. Similarly, for people with severe cognitive impairment due to alcoholic brain damage (Wernicke's encephalopathy and/or Korsakoff's psychosis), further consumption will only increase the damage.

Abstinence is also indicated in the following situations:

- Where someone has made numerous unsuccessful attempts to control their drinking in the past.

- Where the assessment indicates a high level of dependence.

- Where withdrawal symptoms have included DTs (delirium tremens) and/or convulsions.

• Where the individual's desire is abstinence.

If you are experiencing any or all of the above, then you are strongly advised to pursue an abstinence goal rather than reducing or controlling your drinking.

If you feel that you cannot contemplate total abstinence, then try temporary abstinence. Try it for a month, or preferably three months. If you have a couple of months of abstinence behind you, the decision may look very different.

Controlled drinking

Many people addressing a drink problem feel that controlled drinking is the easiest and best option, even though they may have little idea what controlled drinking actually entails. Often people who choose a controlled drinking option believe that somehow it will allow them to continue to enjoy drinking, but to drink in safety. Sometimes they believe that they will be able to drink "normally". However, drinking "normally" usually means not only that there are no restrictions on the drinking or enjoyment but also that there is no need for them.

Controlled drinking means exactly that: the drinking is now controlled. It means that there are certain rules and regulations surrounding drinking. These rules can be those you have set yourself, or they can be the recommendations of doctors and other therapists working in the alcohol field. Whichever you choose, it now means that your drinking is set – a set amount, in a set time. For example, it is recommended that a woman drinks no more than three units and a man no more than four units on any given occasion, that you drink on no more than three or four days a week, and that you drink no more than one drink per hour.

For some people who've been drinking considerable amounts, these restrictions can mean that they no longer enjoy the drinking. Many of them, instead of continuing with controlled drinking, will opt instead for abstinence, which they find easier.

Reduced drinking

Another option that people often prefer to abstinence is reduced drinking. This allows them to continue drinking and retain the positives about alcohol, while eliminating or at least reducing the negatives.

However, if reduced drinking is going to be meaningful, then it needs to be reduced to a level where it no longer causes problems. Again, this means reducing to a level that is considered safe. This takes us back to the recommended limits of three/four units a day and no more than fourteen/twenty-one units a week, so it still retains an element of control.

Of course, you may view these limits as too restrictive and decide instead that *any* reduction must be a positive step. Although this may indeed be true, unless you have a definite plan and set definite limits, you will find that your drinking begins to escalate again. Even if you do decide that reduction is your goal, it is still strongly recommended that you have a period of abstinence prior to starting your reduced drinking goal.

The following chapters assume that you are following an abstinence or temporary abstinence goal. However, if you have decided not to follow that goal and are determined to put a reduced drinking goal into place immediately, you will find some tips on ways to reduce your drinking in Chapter 7.

5

Involving others

You are probably wondering whether you should tell people about stopping drinking. To aid that decision, I have listed some negatives and positives of telling others. These are general suggestions for everyone; you may wish to carry out an analysis that is more specific to you.

The negatives

The first and most obvious reason not to tell others is the shame and stigma attached to being a problem drinker. No one wants to admit that they have a problem with alcohol, or indeed that they have a problem with anything at all. However, the person with the alcohol problem generally seems to be the last to know. Regardless of how clever drinkers think they are, or how well they think they have concealed their drinking, close friends and family are usually well aware of the problem. They may have been wondering for some time how to approach the issue with you. They may have discussed this among themselves but been afraid they would alienate you. So talking to them may free them to approach an issue that has been threatening the relationship.

The second reason is the fear of being shunned by friends or family. This is almost certainly a needless concern.

> Your family will almost certainly already know about your drinking and your struggle. They have probably seen the deterioration as alcohol has become more important to you and they (your friends and family) have become less important. Despite this, they have probably continued to be supportive.

Disclosing may even bring you closer together, as they will want to help you in your struggle to change.

If they have not been supportive, then you have nothing to lose by disclosing. They probably already know about your problems; indeed, it may be that not disclosing or admitting your problem has caused the distance between you. So disclosing now may help to heal that rift.

You may have had a drinking problem for some

considerable time and you may have gone for help or promised to change before. So you may be reluctant to say that you are trying to change again. You may be afraid that people will not believe you – because you understand that they have good reasons not to. You may feel that you will not be taken seriously. This is a difficult situation and you need to try and see things from other people's perspective. You cannot make people believe you. Nevertheless, it is worth pointing out to them that research shows that few problem drinkers change on the first or even second attempt, but the chances of positive change definitely increase if you keep trying, and that is exactly what you are doing – you are still trying to change!

You may feel that if you say out loud that you have a drinking problem, then there is no going back and the world will never be the same again. That is a scary place to be because it entails accepting that you have a problem and need to change. However, if you don't accept the need for change then you are not going to be successful!

A similar reason for wanting to keep quiet is the fear of not being able to change successfully. This is a fear that most people will have at the beginning of any new venture or any kind of change. For you, there may be some nagging doubt because you have tried in the past and were unsuccessful, and you fear that it will be the same result this time. This may or may not be the case. However, if you learn the lessons of where it went wrong in the past, prepare as best you can by building your motivation, plan for the change, stay committed, and follow the hints in this book, you give yourself a very good chance of succeeding this time.

The positives
The first and most important benefit of disclosing your problem to other people is the help and support they can give you. When you feel down or overwhelmed by the effort of change, your friends and family can help to raise your spirits and resolve.

If you are in a situation that involves drinking – for example, at a party, a restaurant, or a celebration – having people there who will look out for you is invaluable. I found that just having them around was very helpful in case my resolve began to weaken. They can act as our conscience when we are not strong; we are much less inclined to drink if there is someone present who knows of our problem.

Disclosure brings people together. It forms a bond of implied trust between them. If, as with many problem drinkers, your relationships have suffered through your drinking, then disclosure can help to heal them. It makes people feel that you are moving towards them and making an effort.

Disclosure is good for you as well. It closes doors for escape, stops you saying to yourself, "I wasn't really that bad," and makes you accountable to those you have disclosed to. You do not want to have to look them in the face and say that you have failed or, worse, that you have not bothered to try.

Of course, the decision as to whether or not to disclose is one that you need to make for yourself. You should definitely be careful how and who you disclose to. Ask yourself whether if by doing so you are harming someone else – for example, it might embarrass a relative who is a public figure. It is also wise not to put yourself at risk – for example, telling your boss if it would mean getting fired. These warnings aside, disclosure is usually a positive step and one that can be very helpful for commitment and, ultimately, for recovery. People generally respect someone who is trying to change much more than someone who continues in their problem!

Do I need to go to AA?

This is another personal decision. Some people love AA and some don't. It is certainly worth checking it out for yourself, as it is difficult to tell who will like it and who won't. One thing that we can probably say with complete certainty is that there are few people who go willingly and joyfully to their first meeting of AA.

If you have no intention of remaining abstinent, then AA is probably not for you. The traditions of AA state, "The only requirement for membership is a desire to stop drinking." So it is probably not a place where someone who is undecided about stopping drinking is going to feel comfortable. If your goal is *temporary*

abstinence, you might still feel comfortable in AA, but that is unlikely.

Recent research into AA has shown that people who were in alcohol treatment and also attended AA had greater success with remaining abstinent than those who did not attend AA. So there is some good evidence that it works.

Where does my doctor fit in?

Your doctor can be a very useful person in the change process. If you are a mildly dependent drinker (experiencing mild withdrawals), then you may need to see your doctor. If you are a moderate, severe, or very severely dependent drinker, then it is strongly recommended that you contact your doctor before starting the change process.

Doctors can be a very good source of support throughout the change process. They can provide emotional support and encouragement, as they have almost certainly helped others through the process. They may also have a Home Detox team that will visit you in your home and provide help, support, and medication. If you are a dependent drinker, then stopping drinking is going to result in withdrawal symptoms. The more dependent you are, the more likely you are to have withdrawals and the more severe they are likely to be.

If you have had DTs or convulsions in the past, you should contact your doctor as a matter of urgency before you stop drinking. Delirium tremens is a medical emergency and can be fatal if not treated properly.

Your doctor can also help with advice about vitamins and minerals. Drinking alcohol can cause depletion of certain vitamins and minerals in your body and this can lead to serious conditions – for example, thiamine is essential for brain function and depletion can lead to irreversible brain damage.

Once you are sober, you may also want to look at your general health, which you may have neglected during the drinking period. You may find that your sleep pattern is disturbed and you find it difficult to get to sleep or stay asleep, or you may experience nightmares. All of these are very common and can be quite distressing in the early days of recovery. Again, a doctor can help you to get through this period.

So, contacting your doctor and having them involved early in the process of change is a sensible move, and, if you are a dependent drinker, essential.

6

Ready, set, go

You have now made most of the important decisions about change and you are now ready to get into action. Let's look at the checklist before going to the next step.

1. You have carried out an assessment   Yes/No
2. You have carried out the motivation exercises Yes/No
3. You have decided on a goal for change – Abstinence/Temporary Abstinence   Yes/No
4. You have decided whether or not to disclose to your family   Yes/No
5. You have decided whether or not to disclose to your friends   Yes/No
6. You have decided whether or not to attend AA Yes/No

> 7. You have decided whether or not to go to your doctor   Yes/No

Setting a date

The next step is to set a date to stop drinking. Obviously this should be as soon as possible and, if there is a medical emergency, it should be immediately. If there is no medical emergency, then you might need to take a few things into consideration. For example, it could be difficult to stop drinking at a time of celebration – birthday, Christmas, or anniversary. Try to set the date for a time when your life will be reasonably quiet and low in stress. If you are employed, it might be worth thinking about stopping when you have a holiday or can take some time off. Then, if you do have withdrawals, at least you will be away from work at the time. On the other hand, if you do not expect to have withdrawals, it might be beneficial to be at work, as this would help to occupy you. (You should still be aware that withdrawals may occur.)

Getting ready

When you have set the date, try and cut down your drinking prior to that date, so that your withdrawals will be reduced. Although it may be tempting, don't have a blow-out the night before you begin your abstinence, because this will only make your withdrawals much worse. You want to make your first day of abstinence as easy as possible.

If you have decided that you are going to disclose to family and/or friends, you should do so before your abstinence start date. You will want as much support as possible during these early days and weeks, so get them on board from the start.

If you are planning to attend AA, then it is wise to make contact beforehand. You can find them online or in your local phonebook. Phone the local contact, who will tell you the time and place of the meetings, and, if you wish, arrange for someone to come to your house and take you to the meeting. If you do not want anyone coming to the house, then they can arrange to meet you somewhere else or at least be there at the meeting to welcome you and introduce you to the other members. This is an invaluable service, as you may feel strange and awkward at first and the person who meets you will know how you feel.

You may also want to look on the internet for support. There are AA meetings online and chat rooms that provide support to problem drinkers. One website that may be useful is www.247helpyourself.com, which I created to help people with an alcohol problem. Some of the techniques and exercises discussed in this book and many others besides can be found at this website, together with a thriving community of people trying to change their drinking habits. It is free for anyone to use.

You should also contact your doctor and fill them in on your plans. They may be able to organize support from the Home Detox team and, if you are showing signs of dependency, can help you with medication that will take the edge off any withdrawals that you may experience.

Prior to the day of change you should stock up on a few items that will make your first few days easier to cope with. If you suffer withdrawals, then you need to keep hydrated, so get in plenty of soft drinks. This is not a week to worry about your weight, and sweet drinks tend to be better at helping with cravings.

Stock up on favourite foods. You may find, particularly if you have been drinking heavily for some time, that you have no appetite. It is also very common to experience sickness and diarrhoea as the toxins from alcohol leave the body. If you can eat, then eat. If not, drink plenty of fluids. This stage will pass.

Get something to keep you entertained. It is common in the early days of abstinence to feel that time is dragging. So having some magazines and DVDs can help pass the time. Remember, especially during the first week, you might have difficulty concentrating, so reading a book or solving puzzles could feel impossible. Again, this is quite normal and your concentration should come back.

Finally, make sure that you have everything you might need and that you haven't forgotten anything – especially something that might entail a trip to the corner shop that sells alcohol. Avoid that temptation. If you have any booze in the house, it would be a very good idea to get rid of it. If you can't because it belongs to someone else, then ask them to put it where you will not be able to see it and be tempted by it.

Now you are ready for the big day!

Day 1

On the first day of change...
- Allow yourself to sleep late if you can.
- Read your motivation cards and keep them close at hand so you can read them regularly through the day.
- Try and have people around who will help and support you, but not irritate you. Tell them what you want/need from them.
- Drink lots of fluids (obviously no alcohol).
- Eat if you can; don't if you can't.
- If you feel like it, take a walk. Have someone accompany you and avoid any shops that sell booze. Leave your money and credit cards at home.
- Watch TV and DVDs, and read magazines to help pass the time.
- If you feel drowsy during the day, try not to sleep – save it for night time.
- Go to bed early and try to sleep. If you can't sleep, don't worry. Your normal sleep pattern will return in time.

You might have to repeat this pattern for a few days, depending on your level of dependence and the extent of the withdrawals. Withdrawals normally last between three and five days, although occasionally they can last longer. You should feel much better physically after the first week. You should congratulate yourself at having achieved a week of abstinence. This is no mean achievement and, depending on your style of drinking, may just be the longest you have gone without a drink for a considerable time.

Now you need to stay stopped. In Chapter 8 we will turn to the subject of relapse and how to avoid it. In the meantime, we will look at reducing consumption.

7

Reducing consumption

You have carried out the assessments in Chapters 1 and 2 and decided that reducing alcohol consumption is the best course of action for you. For this strategy to work you need to do a bit of planning. This chapter will take you through the various steps that you should follow to make sure that you successfully reduce your drinking to a level where it no longer causes problems.

Reducing consumption can be difficult, especially if you do not have a clear idea of how you intend to achieve it. So you need to plan carefully. How much are you going to drink on any one occasion, or in a week; how many abstinent days do you intend to have? How are you going to handle offers of drinks from other drinkers; what are you going to tell them?

These are all questions you need to think about and answer before you can be successful.

Finding your pattern of drinking

The first task is to look at the drinking diary that you completed in Chapter 1. If this is an accurate representation of your typical drinking week, then it should show you the pattern of your drinking: the days you do drink and the days you don't, the days you drink too much. On the days when you drink too much:

- Does this drinking happen at particular times?

- Does it take place in a particular venue?

- Does it take place during certain activities?

- Does it involve particular people?

For example, it may be that on Friday you meet Chris and go to the pub and drink heavily till closing time. On Saturday you go to the football match with Chris and Tom, and afterwards you go to the pub until closing time and you drink heavily. On Sunday you meet Tom and again go to the pub, but you only have four units that day. Does this mean that when you meet Chris you always drink heavily, but you do not always drink heavily when you meet Tom?

It is important to recognize the risky situations so that you can plan for them. The risks may be events (the football), times (Saturday), people (Chris), or places (a particular pub). Once you have identified the risks, you can plan how to handle them.

An obvious way to handle a risk would be to avoid it completely, but that might not be easy if you have established patterns of behaviour – Saturday football, then the pub. Think of ways to alter your routine. For example, instead of going to the pub after the football, go for a meal, or arrange to go somewhere else later, so that you can only stay in the pub for a limited time.

The point is that you are going to have to make changes in your life and your habits. In order to do that, you might have to disclose your intentions to others, especially if you have well-established routines or drinking patterns. Read the section in Chapter 5 about disclosure. What will your response be when someone offers to buy you a drink? Are you going to join in the round-buying?

Tips for reducing alcohol consumption
Here are some tips and pointers as to how you can reduce your drinking under different drinking conditions.

General tips

- Plan to keep within the overall weekly drinking limits (fourteen units for a female and twenty-one for a male).

- Plan to have at least two days a week without alcohol.

- Have long drinks instead of shorts; better still, drink beer or low-alcohol drinks.

- If you are already a beer drinker, drink shandy or low-alcohol beer.

- Pace your drinks and take smaller sips. Consume no more than one drink an hour.

- Don't mix your drinks (for example, beer and spirits).

- Drink for the taste, rather than for the effect.

- Have non-alcoholic drinks in between your alcoholic drinks.

- Don't hold your glass in your hand all the time; if you put it down between drinks, you'll drink less.

Mythbuster

Drinking beer is less intoxicating than drinking wine or spirits.
No! Although it's a good idea to stick to long drinks rather than shorts, all forms of alcohol are intoxicating: half a pint of beer is equivalent to a glass of wine or a normal spirit measure.

At home

- The measures you pour at home are more generous than you get in a bar, so pour less.

- Drink low-alcohol beer or wine or, better still, non-alcoholic drinks.

Before going out

- Mentally prepare yourself for the night ahead. Remind yourself of your decision to change and why you made that decision. The more prepared you are the easier it will be.

- Set rules about the number of drinks you're going to have and stick to that number. Decide that you are going to have no more than one unit per hour and that you will alternate with soft drinks.

- Delay the first drink of the evening by going out later. The longer you delay, the less time you will have for drinking. But don't drink faster to try and make up for lost time! Remember, if you are reducing the time available for drinking, then it is easier to do this by going out later than by coming home earlier. Once we have had a drink, our thinking changes and our best intentions are more difficult to keep.

- Don't drink on an empty stomach. Have a large meal. This stops the alcohol being absorbed into the bloodstream so quickly.

Night out or party

- A night out or a party can be a difficult time to reduce your drinking, especially at the beginning of the process. If possible, take someone with you who knows that you are reducing your drinking and is willing to support you. Discuss what you will do if you feel that it is getting difficult to avoid drinking heavily. One way to handle this is to leave early: make sure that your supporter is happy to leave with you if necessary, and make sure that you are always aware of where that person is in the party.

- In company, people imitate the drinking speed of others, so make sure that you imitate the speed of the slowest drinker, not the fastest.

- Don't buy rounds. Round-buying usually increases the number of drinks that someone has. If you feel that you can't escape the round-buying ritual, then alternate between alcoholic and soft drinks.

- Learn to refuse a drink when offered. Think of a good reason to refuse – for example, "I need to get up early tomorrow." Or make a joke of it – "Whoa, they are coming a bit fast for me tonight!"

- Tell your friends that you are cutting down your drinking. It will be very difficult for you if you don't tell your regular drinking companions that you are trying to cut down.

- Stay away from people who give you a hard time about not drinking as much as they do. You need friends who will support you during this time. If someone is not supporting you, then you need to ask yourself how much of a friend that person is.

• If you feel that your resolve is weakening, don't try to tough it out. Leave! It is not weakness to walk away; it is strength.

If you don't manage to keep to your rules and you drink more than you intended, then learn from it. Why do you think it happened? Did you prepare enough before going out? Did something unexpected happen, which you can learn from and prepare for next time? Don't spend your time feeling guilty and give up trying. Instead, use the experience to ensure a more positive outcome next time.

Reducing alcohol consumption is difficult at the beginning, but it does get easier with time. After a while you will find that your attitude to drinking is changing, and you will find that your attitude towards *you* – and the attitudes of others towards you – is changing as well.

8

Avoiding relapse

Stopping drinking is only the first step on the way to change. The second step is staying stopped. When we look at the statistics for treated problem drinkers, the first thing that strikes us is the appalling relapse rate (anything from 50 to 90 per cent). So why is that?

If you were to ask the general public of non-problem drinkers what is the most difficult thing a problem drinker can do, they would almost certainly say "stop drinking". But they would be wrong! Yes, it is difficult to stop, but staying stopped is almost certainly more difficult.

That's the bad news. The good news is that it gets easier the longer you do it. Statistics show three months to be the time when abstinence becomes stable. That means that once someone has reached three months of abstinence, they are more likely to reach a year than to relapse. Furthermore, those who reach two years are unlikely to relapse again, although they are not immune and continued vigilance is needed.

There is no need for anyone who has stopped drinking to become a recluse or a social leper. It does seem in this current age that much social activity revolves around alcohol or at least has alcohol readily available. This may be an exaggeration, but to the newly abstinent it can seem that alcohol is everywhere. And so the world can feel a bit hostile. It takes time to become comfortable with your new status as a non-drinker and at ease in situations where alcohol is both served and encouraged. Let me reassure you: given time, you will be much more comfortable and your attitude to alcohol will change quite dramatically. You may not believe that now, but one day you will look back and see the difference. In order to get to that day, however, you need to remain abstinent and avoid relapse. Let's look at some strategies and exercises to help you achieve that.

Avoiding temptation

The most obvious strategy is to avoid alcohol. If possible, don't keep it in the house. This might be difficult if you live with others and they like to have a drink. However, you can ask them to keep it away from you and not to drink when you are around. The responsibility not to drink is yours – no one can make you drink – but if your friends and family are being supportive, they should be happy not to drink around you. Besides, they may reap some of the benefits, or at least have fewer problems, if you are no longer drinking.

For the first three months at least you should avoid going into pubs or clubs – anywhere, in fact, where the main activity is drinking. You might feel that you can handle going to pubs earlier, but it can put you under a lot of pressure and that could lead to wanting to drink. If you do go to pubs and are able to handle it, beware the hangover effect – you don't actually feel much pressure at the time, but afterwards there is a build-up of pressure that seems to come from nowhere. In fact, the origin was the pub visit; you just suppressed it at the time.

Although avoiding temptation is a good strategy, particularly in the early days of abstinence, you cannot avoid coming into contact with alcohol for the rest of your life. That's just not realistic. You'll need to adopt other strategies that will allow you to handle alcohol-related situations such as parties and celebrations.

Be prepared
One day someone – perhaps a stranger, perhaps a friend or relative – is going to offer you a drink. What are you going to do or say? If you have never thought about this scenario, then you are going to be taken by surprise. This could be difficult for you and you may

feel that there is social pressure to drink. So instead of being taken by surprise, it is wise to think through the situation, decide what you are going to say, and even rehearse the response.

If you can find someone you are comfortable with, you could use role play, in which your friend is the person offering you a drink. You can then rehearse the responses you are going to make. It may seem awkward and embarrassing, but it is certainly less embarrassing than getting it wrong and starting to drink again.

It's a bit easier if you are offered a drink by a stranger. They have no history of knowing you as a drinker. You can then say, in all honesty, "I don't drink." Rehearse saying that a few times to see if you feel comfortable. If you do, then that can become your stock answer to strangers. "I don't drink." If people ask why you don't drink, then again you can say, in all honesty, "It doesn't agree with me."

If you feel uncomfortable saying you don't drink, you could use other reasons why you are not drinking. For example, "I don't drink when I'm driving" or "I have a bit of a bug at the moment so I'm not drinking" or "I'm taking some medication so I'm not drinking".

Most people do not care whether you drink or not. But you do! So prepare in advance a response that you will feel comfortable with when someone offers you a drink.

It's more difficult when you meet someone you know well or with whom you drank. Unless they know that you have stopped, they may expect you to have a drink with them. So what are you going to say when they offer you a drink? You could be perfectly honest and disclose that you have been having problems and that you have stopped or are giving it a rest for a few months. If they are a true friend, then they will have your welfare at heart and will support and respect your decision. If, on the other hand, they are only interested in you as a drinking companion, they will try and persuade you to have a drink. They might tell you, "You're not really that bad," or, "You were just going through a bad patch," or, "I drink the same as you and I'm OK." Some, but not all, of these drinking friends will have doubts about their own drinking behaviour and see you as a threat to their drinking. If you can do it, then they can and should do it – and they don't want to. Unfortunately, the only answer to these friends is to avoid them.

Avoiding your friends and drinking companions might be difficult. You could argue that these are your friends and have been for years, and you cannot just let them go and not speak to them. But you are on a new journey. You are changing your life and that takes effort and resolve. If your friends and former drinking companions are prepared to help and support you, and meet somewhere where there is no alcohol involved, then great – continue that friendship. This would be a meaningful friendship where you are valued for who you are, and your decisions and goals are respected. If, however, they just want you to go back and drink with them, then you have to ask yourself how much of a friend they are. Perhaps remaining abstinent and becoming an example is the best course of action for you *and* them. One day they might come to you to help them, especially when they see that you are making a real go of abstinence and getting on with a fruitful life. But, for now, you might have to let them go in case they lead you back into the drinking behaviour that you are trying to escape.

Why do you drink?

If you are going to avoid relapse, then you need to be prepared, and, in order to do that, you need to know a bit about your reasons for drinking. You might say that there is no mystery – you drink because you like it, you enjoy it. However, you need to discover what it is about drinking that you enjoy. For example, perhaps you enjoy the taste, the euphoric feeling it gives you, or perhaps it makes you feel better when you are angry. If your enjoyment of drinking comes from the fact that it helps you to cope with your feelings, then this is probably one of your main reasons, or motivations, for drinking. When you become angry, sad, depressed (or whatever feeling alcohol helped you cope with), then you will have a greater desire, or craving, to drink when these feelings arise. A craving can be an uncomfortable feeling – anxiety, or a nervy feeling in your stomach – and it will be a feeling that you associate with wanting a drink.

This type of craving is quite common. We learn to associate alcohol (or any other substance) with a certain situation, for example: feel depressed – drink alcohol – feel better.

This is a form of self-medication very similar to self-medicating for a physical ailment. For example: have a headache – take analgesic – headache gone.

Other associations you may have could be with a person or a place or a time. For example, if every time you met James you had a drink, then you would come to associate him with drinking. Similarly, if every time you went to a certain place you had a drink, then again you would associate that place with drinking. This may seem obvious: if you went to the King's Head pub and you met James, then, of course, that would be why you were there – to have a drink. But it is also the more subtle, subconscious changes that can make it difficult for you to refuse a drink in these circumstances.

If you regularly go drinking at 7 p.m. on a Friday, then an association is made between this time and drinking. Your mind and your body are accustomed to having alcohol and feeling different at this time. If you have stopped drinking, when Friday 7 p.m. comes around, your body is not getting its "fix" and so it reacts. How exactly it reacts is different for each individual, but most people will interpret the reaction as craving. Your mind and body are missing the alcohol and they want it![1]

The point is not to prevent it happening, because you can't. The point is to be prepared for it and to have a plan as to how you are going to handle it when it does happen. So the first thing is to make a note of where, when, and under what circumstances these cravings occur. Keep a diary or a notebook and write down when the craving happens so that you can look for patterns and anticipate them. Do they occur at the same time or in the same place? Do they happen when you meet a particular person or when you are in a particular mood? The more you know about your enemy – the craving – the better.

> Craving reaches a peak at around twenty minutes and lasts only thirty-five minutes. If you can delay drinking for thirty-five minutes, you will beat the craving.

1. This craving is due to the learning process called conditioning. Pavlov found that his dogs salivated when they were given food. This was their preparation for eating and digesting the food. He then found that if he rang a bell just before he gave them food, after doing this a few times the dogs would be conditioned to salivate on hearing the bell. In a similar way, humans begin to associate places, people, and times with drinking, and our body makes adjustments which we may interpret as excitement or anticipation of the alcohol. Thus, when we are in these places, with these people, or it is that time, our body makes the adjustments. But now, because there is no alcohol, we call it craving.

When a craving occurs, it feels powerful and endless, but that is not the case: cravings have limitations. A craving for alcohol is like a wave: it starts slowly, builds to a peak, and then crashes on the shore and disappears. Research shows us that craving reaches a peak in about twenty minutes and then starts to diminish over the next fifteen minutes. So a craving will last, start to finish, for around thirty-five minutes. If you can last that long, then the craving will pass.

> Research also shows us that if you continually resist a craving, then over time it will diminish – that is, it will become weaker and less able to affect you. Conversely, if you give in to a craving, it becomes harder to resist next time.

So how do you resist cravings until they pass?

- One way is by **urge surfing** – gritting your teeth and realizing that although it may be unpleasant and uncomfortable, it can't actually harm you. Some treatment centres teach this type of technique because it helps the client to build their confidence to resist cravings and so remain abstinent.

- A second way is to engage in some **distracting activity**. Reading, a hobby, going to a movie, and exercising (jogging, cycling) are good examples. Once you get interested in something else, you'll find the urges go away.

- Another effective response to craving is **eating**. Most people don't feel like drinking after eating a big meal or something very sweet. This should not be considered a long-term strategy because it substitutes one substance for another, but as a short-term solution it is fine.

- **Talking it through** is another strategy. You could talk to friends or family members about craving when it occurs. If you have joined AA, this is where other members can be helpful because they know exactly what you are talking about, having been there themselves. Talking about cravings and urges can be very helpful in pinpointing the source of the craving. Talking also often helps to discharge and relieve the feeling and will help restore honesty in your relationship. Craving is nothing to feel bad about. You can use the internet and go to an online forum to talk through your cravings and get support from others in the community (for example, the 24/7 Help Yourself community).

If you are someone who tends to drink to cope with their feelings, then talking through how you are feeling is a good relapse-prevention strategy. Many people, particularly men, have difficulty expressing how they feel and take refuge in alcohol. But if this is one of your main triggers for drinking, then you need to find an alternative. Like most things, it gets easier the more you practise.

Don't forget that cravings pass, and doing something distracting will make them pass more quickly!

9
What if I do slip?

It is possible that you may give in to temptation. You would not be the first and you certainly won't be the last. Unfortunately, relapse is all too common in problem drinking. It is helpful to understand that change is a process, not an event. So remember the words of the old cliché – if at first you don't succeed, try, try, and try again. Nevertheless, you need to manage the situation so that you do not lose the benefits of all your good work.

Just because you slip does not mean you have to continue drinking. You can stop again any time you choose. You have the choice!

The first thing you need to do is prevent the situation from escalating. There is a big difference between taking one drink, or even a few drinks, and getting drunk for a week. (Alan Marlatt, an American psychologist, talks about lapse and collapse.) So try to stop immediately, or as soon as you possibly can. You should have a phone number of someone you trust and who will support you – a relative, a friend, or an AA member. Use this number and get help from them. If necessary, ask them to come and get you or come and be with you.

Your pride and confidence will have taken a pretty large blow. Feelings of uselessness are common in these circumstances. Unfortunately, it is in these very circumstances and to relieve these very feelings that many problem drinkers have been used to drinking heavily. You need to avoid that now by using any coping mechanism at your disposal – distraction, talking to someone, anything that is effective for you. Again, this feeling will pass.

Getting back on track

This is not a time for guilt and beating yourself up. This is a time when you need to look at the positives of the situation, not the negatives. Have you reduced your drinking – the amount, the frequency? You have had a slip, but did you stop more quickly than you would normally have stopped? Are you back on track? Is your resolve to stop drinking still strong? Look at your "reasons for stopping" card.

Once you have stopped drinking again, you should return to your routine. Build and maintain your motivation, and use your motivation card every morning. If you joined AA, get back to the meetings as quickly as you can. You may be wondering whether you should tell people what happened. It is strongly advisable that you do tell them. If you don't tell them, you will feel guilty, and your guilt will make your relationships with the other members awkward and you may then want to avoid them. This would deny you the support that you have built up, and without that you might end up drinking again. Remember, you would be telling them what happened in order to help yourself, not to humiliate yourself or to confess. You would be telling them so that you feel able to call on them for support, which would be difficult if you had lied to them or kept back information.

It is also important afterwards to look at what you have learned from the situation. Could it have been avoided? Was there anything you were doing that you should not have been doing? For example, were you putting yourself at risk by going to a pub too early in your recovery, or when you were in a low mood? Was there anything you should have been doing that you weren't? Had you stopped your morning routine of reading your reasons for change? Had you stopped attending AA meetings or sharing your feelings?

This is a time for ruthless honesty. You do not want to keep repeating the same mistake; it will erode your confidence and the confidence of your supporters. You also need to be realistic. You can't expect that those closest to you will not be disappointed. All their hopes of you stopping drinking, for your sake and for theirs, will be in tatters at the moment. They will need time to get back on your side.

Put yourself in their place for a moment: how would you feel if the situations were reversed? They may need to see some proof that you are seriously trying to change again. This will be especially true if you have a history of promising change and then relapsing. It may be difficult for them to come on board completely again. Give them time; if you show them you are serious, they will start to believe it again.

Can I ever drink again?

If you are not a dependent drinker, then there is a good possibility that you could drink again in safety. However, most treatment agencies would say that the more dependent on alcohol you are, the less likely that a return to moderate social drinking is an option.

For people who are dependent and severely dependent, this is a difficult question, and unfortunately the only sensible answer is: no one can possibly know. Many people believe that problem drinking – in particular alcoholism (or dependent drinking) – is a disease and that it is progressive. What this means is that even if you have stopped drinking, the disease continues to grow in severity. People who

support this model of alcoholism would adamantly say that there is no way you could drink again in safety.

> Would you want to risk all that you have achieved for a drink? It is a huge gamble. You might be able to drink again, but you might have all the problems that you had before – and more.

Leaving aside the question of whether or not dependent drinking is a disease and whether or not it is progressive, there is no doubt that many, if not most, dependent drinkers seem to be incapable of drinking again in a moderate manner. Whether this is, as some would argue, rooted in the drinker's physical make-up, or, as others believe, has a psychological basis, is still debated hotly.

Maybe "Can I drink again?" is the wrong question. Instead, perhaps the question should be "Would I want to take the risk of drinking again?" If you have managed to stop drinking for some months or even years, would you want to jeopardize all that you have gained for a drink? Look back at the pros and cons exercise that you carried out in Chapter 3. Would you want to risk having the cons of drinking back in your life? Is your life so miserable now you have stopped drinking that you would go back to drinking, or is that a gamble too far? This time you do have a choice, something you did not have when you were drinking. I have that choice, and today it is far too risky for me to drink again. Even on bad days – and I have had some (I have been divorced and have buried people close to me) – I still prefer to be sober.

10

Looking forward

You have now been sober for three months and you have decided to remain abstinent. Despite your earlier preconceptions, you have decided that returning to drinking is just too great a risk. It could jeopardize all that you have achieved and built. You wish to stay sober and have a more fulfilled life than you had when you were drinking. This chapter discusses some of the issues that you will need to address if you are going to have a happy and contented sobriety.

The family (1)

Living life without alcohol can be a real adventure. In sobriety you see the world in a different way. People often talk about having the blindfold taken off. They describe being more alive than they have been for years, wanting to do things – to travel, to experience, to achieve.

The family will usually welcome this change. They see that their father/mother/wife/husband is now sober and living a much more healthy and productive life. Sometimes, however, sobriety does not always bring the happiness and closeness that the family dreamed of. Newly sober people can be enthusiastic about their new life and expect their close friends and family to share that enthusiasm.

Unfortunately, for family members who want a return to "normal family life" without the drinking, the new-found enthusiasm and new interests can make them feel as if they have "lost" their relative again. An example of this could be a love of AA. AA can be very helpful, but some new members go to meetings on every available occasion, leaving the family feeling justifiably neglected.

This over-enthusiastic adoption of new interests is not confined to AA meetings. One newly sober husband and father wanted to lose weight and get fit, so he started cycling. He spent increasing amounts of his time and money on cycling. He trained every evening, and every weekend he went for long rides with the club. His family, although happy that he was no longer drinking, felt that they had actually had more of his company when he was drinking. Eventually, there was a confrontation and he reduced his cycling, realizing that he had been rather insensitive.

It is worth remembering that your family will often have suffered, or at least been neglected, during your drinking days and they are looking forward to a stable family life. The new life you discover may be seductive, but be sensitive to the needs of your family.

The family (2)

Getting sober can be a turbulent and unsettling time, especially if you have been drinking heavily for years. Changing your life so fundamentally can make you question everything: your values, your attitudes, your status (for example, your job or finances), your friendships, and even your marriage. Although this is another natural and common part of the process of change, it is nevertheless important to get a sense of perspective, particularly if you are feeling dissatisfied.

Find someone you trust and respect whom you can share with. If you are a member of AA, find a sponsor or someone who has been sober for a long time; otherwise, choose a close friend whom you feel you can talk to, or even find a counsellor. Be as open and honest as you can about how you are feeling and thinking. Whatever you do, make a decision not to make important changes in your life based on your feelings until you have talked things through with someone or at least given them considerable thought.

Moods

Most people who give up drinking notice that they have mood swings, sometimes rapid and seemingly uncontrollable. This does not necessarily mean that you have a mood disorder. There can be a number of underlying causes. First, alcohol was quite probably your way of handling normal frustration, anger, or any other negative emotion. Now that you do not drink, you are beginning to experience the emotions that you had previously numbed with booze. Second, you might always have been moody but drinking has masked it. Now that you are sober, you are rediscovering your personality. Finally, getting sober can leave you feeling emotionally exposed, vulnerable, and raw so that trivial incidents can provoke a disproportionate reaction.

If these mood swings continue months into sobriety, you should talk to your doctor about them. For most people, however, this is just another part of getting sober. One of the main emotions you will feel is anger. You may find yourself exploding about nothing and/or taking offence even when no offence was intended.

For most people this "edginess" disappears over time as they remain sober; nevertheless, if ignored, it can cause problems in relationships. Now that drinking is not an option, you need to learn ways of dealing with your emotions that are not destructive. Here are a few suggestions.

- **Exercise** helps to burn off some of the pent-up aggression and anxiety, and so may reduce the outbursts of anger.

- **Going for a walk**, as well as being a good form of the exercise, gives you "time out" from the source of irritations.

- **Meditation** or **prayer** helps to calm the mind.

- **Think before you speak** – the clichéd "Count to ten" and "Take a deep breath" do work.

- **Pursue a hobby that suits you** – play golf, go fishing, paint, take up gardening.

There is no definitive answer to controlling your emotions; do whatever suits you and helps you keep them under control.

Guilt

Many drinkers will have done things or not done things as a result of their drinking that leave them feeling ashamed and guilty. It is difficult to live comfortably if you are full of guilt; indeed, for many drinkers, guilt might have been a prime motivation for drinking, because it allowed them to "forget".

One way to deal with guilt is to make a list of everyone you have hurt and, provided it does not harm you or someone else, say you are sorry. If the person is a family member, then you could try making amends.

One of the most powerful ways of making amends is to stay sober. You should also remember that one of the people you have probably hurt the most is yourself, so include yourself in the list. Part of the AA programme is designed to deal with guilt. Members are urged to make amends to people they have harmed, to apologize and try to make things right.

Regret

Regret can be experienced when we realize that there are things we might have done or achieved that we did not. For example, you might feel that you could have advanced more in your career than you have done, or you might have gone to university, travelled, or told someone that you loved them. Many regrets can be resolved now you are sober, but some cannot.

> You can never turn the clock back and relive your life. You can't go back and do everything that you would like to, but there are some things that you can do. You could become a better husband, wife, father, brother, sister, friend, son, daughter. It is not too late to change that aspect of your life.

Now that you are sober you have time and an opportunity to reinvent yourself. Provided you are realistic, there is much you can do. You could learn a new skill, a new hobby, take up a sport; find out what motivates you.

Helping others

Many ex-drinkers feel that they now have something to give to others who have drink problems. This may or may not be true, but it is certainly often a common desire. Helping others takes skill, empathy, and training. It also takes commitment and stable sobriety. If you feel that you want to train as an alcohol or drug counsellor, then most courses have a policy regarding users and drinkers. Many of them will require you to have been clean and sober for a minimum of two years. This is not only to protect the you from taking on too much too soon; it also protects clients from being exposed to therapists who are still working through their own issues.

Depression and grief

Depression is a common complaint among ex-drinkers. However, although it is more common in this group, clinical depression requiring treatment is still relatively rare. If you continue to have low mood, low appetite, feelings of worthlessness, low energy, and sleep disorders, then contact your doctor. What is more common, but less well recognized, is grief. The drinker can be grieving for a "friend" (alcohol) that comforted them when they were troubled, or that they associate with good times. Like all grieving processes, it can take time to pass. Finding new sober pursuits can help.

You are now free of the physical addiction of alcohol. The choices you make today are sober choices based on what you want in your life. This can be a new beginning and it can be exciting, a new chance to make the kind of life that you want for you and your family. Don't endure it – enjoy it.

For the family

This chapter is for the family of the drinker, to give them a few pointers. In no way is it a complete discussion of the topic or a comprehensive help guide for family. And it only covers the time when the drinker is trying to get sober; for advice on living with a problem drinker who is not trying to get sober, I recommend my book *Bottled Up*.

If your drinker is reading this book, then you probably have a mixture of feelings. On the one hand, you are probably happy that they appear to be putting some action into addressing their alcohol problem, but you are probably also quite anxious in case they do not follow through. You may even feel guilty that you don't entirely trust them – you want to, dearly want to, but you can't. You can't trust them because you have been here before; your hopes have been built up and shattered, maybe many times. This, unfortunately, is the nature of addiction; it is also the nature of recovery.

> Change is a process, not an event. Research suggests that, on average, drinkers relapse three times before they finally change. So hang in there.

People who are addicted to any substance or behaviour may try to change many times before they actually succeed. Think about your own experience: have you ever gone on a diet, decided that you would start an exercise programme? How long did you last and how often have you tried? This is not to make excuses; it is just trying to get a perspective on the situation. When trying to change behaviour, people try and people fail. The good news is that they also succeed, but it may take time and more than one attempt.

So, rather than feel guilty about not believing the person you are supporting, think of it as having a healthy scepticism based on what you know about change. Try and be happy that they are trying to change, without setting your sights too high. View any progress as positive and use it to encourage them to keep trying. That's what they want from you now – your support!

You are not to blame

You are not to blame for someone else's drinking or if they relapse. That is their issue and they need to take responsibility for it. You are not their keeper. It is not your responsibility to keep them sober, but it is in your best interest to support them in any way you can.

It is worth reading Chapter 10, especially the parts about mood swings and decisions. It is important for you to understand that the outbursts are not about you personally. These are their inner struggles. People who are in the midst of change can feel very raw and vulnerable emotionally; this means that they feel as if they have little control over their life. Many people, when vulnerable, use emotions that make them feel powerful and in control. Anger is one of these emotions. It gives a feeling of power and deflects the mind away from the anxieties and insecurities that they are feeling.

Regardless of what they are doing and why they are doing it, it is still very uncomfortable if you are the apparent target of that anger. It is particularly uncomfortable (not to say unfair) if you have been supporting them during their change, as well as having been there throughout their drinking time. You have every right to feel hurt and unappreciated. There will be time for you to express that hurt, but this is not that time! Try to hang on in there and be supportive. Keep telling yourself that if they successfully change, it will benefit you too.

This does not mean that you should become the passive target of their emotional turmoil. They need to deal with their anger (refer them to Chapter 10), not take it out on their family. Try not to get sucked into a full-blown argument. You will both be very sensitive at this stage of the change process and a full-blown argument could bring up long-held hurts and disappointments. This could be very destructive and could give them an excuse to drink and further widen the gulf between you.

If they want to vent their anger, and you feel that you can listen without reacting too much, it could be very helpful to them and could help your relationship in the long term. However, if you can't listen without reacting, don't feel guilty about it – it can feel very uncomfortable and unfair. Instead, try to walk away and leave them to deal with their anger.

Other ways of supporting

Although their drinking is most definitely their problem, remember that you do have a stake in them stopping drinking. If they are staying sober, it will reduce your anxiety and uncertainty about whether they will get drunk tonight, whether you can make plans or if they will be sabotaged again. So be pragmatic and decide that if you can help in this change process, then it is in the interests of both of you to do so.

If they decide to go for help elsewhere – their doctor, AA, or an alcohol treatment unit – they might want you to go with them. It could be helpful for you to go, as it might mean that they actually get there and it will save you from worrying. It could also help your relationship.

Get support

The first few weeks and months of stopping drinking are undoubtedly a difficult time for them. It is also a very difficult time for you. Some family members have described it as "walking on eggshells", as they feel that they have to tiptoe, emotionally and sometimes literally, around them. This takes its toll on you as the supporter. You may feel, on the one hand, that you are being asked to do too much and that it is all a bit unfair, and, on the other hand, guilty that you are not fully trusting them or doing more.

For these reasons it is advisable that you get support for yourself. Find someone you can share your feelings with, someone you feel comfortable with and who will not judge you, but who is also impartial. Support could come from family or friends. Or if you can think of no one who fills the above criteria, you could try a counsellor, who would be impartial. Unfortunately, there is not the same level of support for the families of drinkers; in fact, there is almost no support available in the statutory sector.

You could try Al-Anon, the family groups of Alcoholics Anonymous. These are mutual support groups of people who live with problem drinkers. They meet on a regular basis and follow a modified version of the 12 Step programme. You can find a number for your local Al-Anon group at the front of your phonebook.

A new mostly web-based group is Bottled-up, which I created with my wife Lou. This brand new programme is a combination of science and personal experience. You can find this group at http://bottled-up.memberlodge.com.

> *Remember that this is a great opportunity to be a family again, to have a sober relationship. You need to recognize that you might have to make changes yourself. The relationship with a sober person is very different from the one with a drinker and it will be a learning experience for both of you. However, it can also be the beginning of a great adventure together.*
>
> *Good luck.*

Useful resources

Websites to help with problem drinking
www.247helpyourself.com
www.alcoholhelponline.com
www.aa.org

Websites for information about problem drinking
www.niaaa.nih.gov
www.alcohol-and-drug-guide.com

Websites for information help for families
www.bottled-up.memberlodge.com
www.al-anon.alateen.org

Some helpful books
Adams, A.J., *Undrunk: A Skeptic's Guide to AA,* Deerfield, FL: HCI Books, 2009.

Beattie, M., *Codependent No More: How to Stop Controlling Others and Start Caring for Yourself,* Deerfield, FL: HCI Books, 2009.

Carr, A., *Allen Carr's Easy Way to Control Alcohol*, London: Arcturus, 2003.

DeSena, J., *Overcoming Your Alcohol, Drug and Recovery Habits: An Empowering Alternative to AA and 12-Step Treatment*, Tuscon, AZ: See Sharp Press, 2002.

Rotgers, J., Kern, M.F., and Hoeltzel, R., *Responsible Drinking: A Moderation Management Approach for Problem Drinkers,* Oakland, CA: New Harbinger Publications, 2002.Also in the 'First Steps' series:

Also currently available in the "First Steps" series:

First Steps out of Anxiety
Dr Kate Middleton

First Steps out of Depression
Sue Atkinson

First Steps out of Eating Disorders
Dr Kate Middleton
and Dr Jane Smith

Forthcoming in 2011:

First Steps out of Gambling
Lisa Mills and Joanna Hughes

First Steps through Bereavement
Sue Mayfield

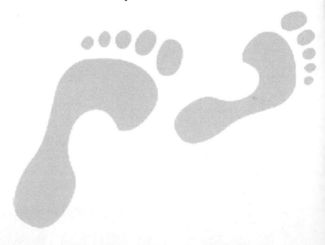